Extraordinary Praise for

It's My Time

"Rev. Kim Y. Neal has a heart for the struggles that persons face every day. Using this devotional will help you refocus your energy on what God says is possible. Read, meditate, and stretch out to see God move in your life in a powerful way."

—**Bishop Walter S. Thomas Sr.**
New Psalmist Baptist Church, Baltimore, MD

"It doesn't take a long time to connect with and respond to God. The Rev. Y. Kim Neal gives practical, real-life, 'me time' opportunities to reach out to and respond to God. I've known Kim for more than three decades. She is transparent, authentic, strongly devoted, and on fire for God. This is a MUST READ for all who want practical steps to a stronger relationship with God, and a deeper spiritual journey. Rev. Kim Y. Neal is REAL."

—**Rev. Dr. Suzan Johnson Cook**
The first female President of the Hampton University Ministers' Conference encourages and helps to empower women leaders. She was the 3rd U. S. Ambassador at Large for International Religious Freedom for President Obama, and a NYC Pastor for 3 decades.

"It is true, one cannot have a sound spiritual foundation without having a consistent and dedicated devotional life. Rev. Kim Y. Neal has demonstrated this principle of life as she reflects on her relationship with God through this 90-day devotional. I encourage anyone to read it, for it contains the very heart of God."

—**Rev. Dr. Lewis N. Watson**
Senior Pastor, First Baptist Church, Salisbury, MD

It's been my wonderful pleasure to have known Rev. Kim Y. Neal for many years. I've always admired her exceptional preaching ability, but in her latest book, It's My Time, I've come to know her ability to inspire and encourage in profound yet practical ways. Reading this powerful devotional just two minutes a day would provide hours of inspiration to a very broad audience. In her own words, "Sometimes God's blessings are not in giving, but in what is taken away." Expect to come away from this brief devotional with fresh wind for your day.

—**Dr. Dwight S. Riddick Sr.**
President of Hampton University Ministers' Conference 2014-2018
Senior Pastor, Gethsemane Baptist Church, Newport News, VA

IT'S MY TIME

IT'S MY TIME

TWO MINUTE DEVOTIONAL IN THE WORD

Rev. Kim Y. Neal

Suffolk, VA

IT'S MY TIME
TWO MINUTE DEVOTIONAL IN THE WORD

Copyright © 2018 by Kim Y. Neal
All rights reserved.

All rights reserved. This book is protected by the copyright laws of the United States of America. This book may not be copied or reprinted for commercial gain or profit. The use of quotations or occasional page copying for personal or group study is permitted and encouraged. Permission will be granted upon request.

Unless otherwise identified, Scripture quotations are from the King James Version. Copyright © 1982 by Thomas Nelson, Inc. Used by permission. All rights reserved.

Final Step Publishing, LLC

PO Box 1441
Suffolk, VA 23439

For Worldwide Distribution
Printed in U.S.A.

Soft cover ISBN: 978-0-9861250-7-2
E-Book ISBN: 978-0-9861250-8-9

Library of Congress Cataloging-in-Publication Data
Names: Neal, Kim Y.
Title: It's my time/Kim Y. Neal;
LCCN: 2018945228
LC record available at https://lccn.loc.gov/2018945228

Cover Design: Lina Imaging Design
Proofreading: Cooke House Publishing, LLC
Inside Cover Design: CMI Leadership Coaching, LLC

DEDICATION

This book is dedicated to my paternal grandmother, Hallie Sallie Cooper Neal, who in my eyes was spiritual nobility.

FOREWORD

Out of her many years of daily meditation on the scripture, Kim Y. Neal shares with us golden nuggets of insight, challenge, and encouragement. Her greatest gift to us is the invitation to honor our own soul by setting aside just a few moments each day to enter into a time of deep communion with God. She shares with us the fruit of her reflections in order to prime the pump of our own listening and responding to the word God sends.

I remember my first year in seminary when a chapel speaker encouraged students to read Psalm 139 for thirty days. I accepted the challenge and it changed my life. It was not only the content of the psalm that was a source of blessing, but the discipline of spending special time in the presence of God, morning by morning.

A valuable feature of these beautiful meditations is the space reserved for writing our own faith responses. In times such as these, with distractions to occupy our time and muddle the voice of the Spirit working in our lives, it is ever more important for such a practice as this. Because of Kim's dedication to living with holy scripture, we are all gifted with a chance to fine tune our hearing and be transformed by the song of the Spirit waiting to break through the chaos of our lives.

What a powerful pastoral gift to be reminded that what God speaks in our own hearts and minds may be the life enriching revelation we need to point us in the direction of greater personal fulfillment and even more effective ministry.

—James A. Forbes, Jr.
Senior Minister Emeritus, The Riverside Church
President and Founder, Healing of the Nations Foundation

INTRODUCTION

One of the most difficult challenges for me is to carve out "me" time. I have long practiced early morning devotionals as that special, daily time with God. In this book you will find two-minute devotionals you can utilize as centering moments to begin each day. Each meditation from the Scripture is a life-leading, life-lifting WORD that will guide you through the day. Your faith will be strengthened and the awareness in the power of your potential will be heightened. You will discern the mysteries of God hidden in the treasure of His Word and discover a wisdom in you that only has to be awakened.

This 90-day devotional gave me an opportunity to explore my personal goals and recalibrate my spiritual life. It is my prayer it does the same for you. A helpful approach to this daily devotional is following the three R's:

READ each devotional and accompanying scripture(s)

REFLECT on the Word of God and its application to your life

RESPOND by writing a lesson learned, a new perspective or something you would like to change.

IT'S MY TIME

I often find it is not until I make permanent documentation (writing) that I become committed to changing the way I think or act.

It's a new day, a new opportunity, and a new you! Embrace this new day to write a new chapter in the story of your life and put into practice all the lessons learned from yesterday. The page is blank in the book of time. This day is your opportunity to renew and reconnect with the God who says "Behold, I will make all things new."

Be Blessed.

Rev. Kim Y. Neal

DAY 1

I will praise thee; for I am fearfully and wonderfully made: marvellous are thy works; and that my soul knoweth right well.
Psalm 139:14

I am God's treasure, uniquely shaped and formed in God's image and the CROWN of God's CREATION. Looking at images of western beauty and masculinity in print media can quickly help you identify something you would like to change about yourself: a thinner nose, broader shoulders, wider hips, fuller lips, or those desirable six-pack abs. Coming to the realization that you are exactly what God had in mind when creating you is both liberating and transformative. Fashion icons say you must look a certain way, but each of us must come to the comfortable conclusion that I love "me" exactly the way God made me.

FAITH RESPONSE:

_____

_____

_____

_____

_____

DAY 2

*This is the day which the L<small>ORD</small> hath made;
we will rejoice and be glad in it.*
Psalm 118:24

A new day is your opportunity to practice what you have learned about life on yesterday. You never have to start over, only start again. The wisdom of starting again should never be daunting. When we start again, we bring with us a new starting point—the wisdom of all our previous attempts. Don't get caught up in the cycle of starting over. Our spirit has memory, so never dismiss or delete lessons learned. Instead of calling them failed attempts, I'll rightly call them learning attempts. Simply call on the wisdom of your past and apply all of your learned knowledge to a new context. This one concept can radically change your life. Rejoice, and be glad in this day.

FAITH RESPONSE:

_____

_____

_____

_____

_____

DAY 3

"And God said ... and there was ..."
Genesis 1:3

Be impeccable with your word. Say what you mean and mean what you say. This one practice is so empowering; it will compel you to think before you speak. Don't be afraid to pause, take a break, take a breath, or take a knee. Whatever you need to do to give yourself time to process your level of commitment, take it. Simply ask, "May I get back with you tomorrow?" Or, sometimes your answer must be NO (Next Opportunity)! Your word alone speaks to your level of integrity. If the meeting is at one in the afternoon, arrive at twelve forty-five. If you have misjudged your time, call ahead and give a new estimated time of arrival. Use the power of your word to build bridges of business and friendship that are long lasting.

FAITH RESPONSE:

_____

_____

_____

_____

_____

DAY 4

"...for he that cometh to God must believe that he is, and that he is a rewarder of them that diligently seek him."
Hebrews 11:6

Hidden spiritual blessings await you if you would search for them with determination. Nothing of any great value comes easily or quickly. When you desire spiritual blessings, you must be prepared to search for them as if searching for a hidden treasure because you are! The scripture reminds us that we have "this treasure in earthen vessels" (2 Corinthians 4:7). Would God place this treasure on the surface of your soul? Absolutely not. Your treasure would easily be tampered with, lost, or stolen. God hides treasure in deep and hidden places within us, so we might search for them and never give up until we find them. The price is high, but the reward is great.

FAITH RESPONSE:

_____

_____

_____

_____

_____

_____

DAY 5

"If we confess our sin, He is faithful to forgive us our sins, and cleanse us from all unrighteousness."
1 John 1:9

Confession is equally as therapeutic a process as psychotherapy. Save the money and confess . . . I DID IT! The psalmist David in Psalm 51 says "I acknowledge my transgressions and my sin is ever before me." After a series of bad decisions and bad consequences, David stops the downward spiral and spiritual falling away by simply saying I did it and I'm sorry. For some, rather than make this type of confession, we medicate ourselves with retail therapy, happy hours, and a broad selection of feel-good entertainment. Here's the truth. We should never feel good when we've done wrong. When we have offended God, ourselves, or someone else, we should be uncomfortable, restless, disquieted, and anxious. Allow the Spirit of God to do the work of the Spirit and allow therapists and other trained mental health care professionals to take care of the other matters.

FAITH RESPONSE:
_____
_____
_____
_____
_____

DAY 6

"... and a threefold cord is not quickly broken."
Ecclesiastes 4:12

Relational issues are complicated. I don't suspect anyone who has experienced divorce went into the marriage relationship with divorce in mind. Many people I have shared intimate conversations with have told me divorce is equivalent to a death. No one goes into a marriage hoping it will end in divorce, but divorce happens. Jesus gives an acceptable justification for divorce (Matthew 19:7-9) but at the end of the day, a death is still a death. The death of a partnership, the death of intimacy, the death of dreams and goals. Whatever reasons the relationship did not survive does not mean you have to die with it. God forgives our failures. Experience God's healing power and choose to live through it and beyond it.

FAITH RESPONSE:

_____

_____

_____

_____

_____

_____

DAY 7

"Yet because this widow troubleth me, I will avenge her, lest by her continual coming she weary me."
Luke 18:5

All of us have faced the end of our strength and resources and we simply wanted to quit. In fact, quitting seemed like a better option than going forward. Living in the Lehigh Valley in Eastern Pennsylvania with my young daughter prepared me for the rise of sudden and severe storms. Once, when leaving New York, after visiting my parents and returning home we ran into one such storm. The torrential rains were blinding, the crashing of the thunder was deafening, and the lightening was a cosmic display of pyrotechnics. My daughter in tears pleaded with me to pull the car over and wait for the storm to pass. I reached into the backseat to test the security of her car seat, held her hand, and simply said to her, "We have to ride this one out." With my heart pounding and left hand shaking on the steering wheel, I said my prayers and continued driving. I had become familiar with these storms and I knew I could ride it out, and we did. So can you. Quitting is not an option. Keep Going.

FAITH RESPONSE:
_____
_____
_____
_____

DAY 8

"I can do all things through Christ which strengtheneth me."
Philippians 4:13

What one woman can do another can do also. I have never invested much energy in negative emotions, particularly a jealous or envious spirit. I've always believed that anyone can accomplish anything with sustained effort and passion. Accomplished men and women were always models to shape my desires, dreams, and goals. The quiet mantra behind every vision for me is "if they could do it, I can do it." Women and men seem to often find themselves competing with their peers, colleagues, their spouses, and sometimes their children. We can better use our energy in a more positive and productive way. Make a conscious decision to refuse to get caught up in the mental and emotional minutiae that infects relationships with a paralyzing venom and simply say, if he can do it, I can do it, and then make it happen.

FAITH RESPONSE:

_____

_____

_____

_____

_____

_____

DAY 9

"But seek ye first the kingdom of God, and his righteousness; and all these things shall be added unto you."
Matthew 6:33

Get rid of the checklist:
    Married by this time
    Get in the right circle of people
    Don't offend this one or that one
    Join this organization
    Get a degree from this school.
    Live in this neighborhood
    Earn this salary.

Just STOP IT!

Allow the Spirit of God to dwell in you richly. Honor God, serve faithfully, and sweet additions will be added to your life.

FAITH RESPONSE:

_____

_____

_____

_____

_____

DAY 10

> *"It is a good thing to give thanks unto the Lord…"*
> **Psalm 92:1a**

God should not have to disrupt your life to get your attention. Give God the attention He deserves. Most of us spend the early part of our morning preparing a list of things we would like to accomplish for the day. Every day should include a time of meditation and reflection on the goodness and grace of God. Every morning, for just a few moments, we should go through our inventory of blessings, past and present, as a reminder of God's beneficence.

Kept my family safe while we slept. Thank you!

Awakened at home and not a hospital. Thank you!

In the hospital and not the morgue. Thank you!

If an inventory of your blessings does not inspire your day, nothing will. God deserves your praise.

FAITH RESPONSE:

_____

_____

_____

_____

DAY 11

"Jesus saith unto him, I am the way, the truth, and the life..."
John 14:6

What have you lost except your illusions? Now start again and build on truth. Some lives have been so scripted by parents and loved ones that you knew the school you would attend, when you would graduate, your confirmed major, the age you would marry, the number of children you would have, and when you would have them, and the list goes on. Our plans, no matter how well laid out they may be can differ from God's plan for our life. If you lost something or someone, let it go. We can exert no more control over our lives than we can control the weather. LET IT GO! Let go of the storyline or the fantasy you've created which held that illusion together for you for so long. It doesn't make sense anymore. Simply LET GO AND LET GOD HAVE HIS WAY. The truth really will set you free.

FAITH RESPONSE:

_____

_____

_____

_____

_____

DAY 12

"Give us this day our daily bread."
Matthew 6:11

I am excited about your RIGHT NOW. We spend so much of our time planning for the future. We plan for college, retirement, marriage, children, lesson plans, financial plans, budgets, weekend plans, and vacations. I often feel like an unpaid event planner in my teenage daughter's life. We can become so focused on tomorrow that we overlook the POWER OF NOW. The power of this moment we have is humbling and awe-inspiring. Jesus taught His disciples to pray daily: "Give us THIS day, our daily bread." With just this one affirmation, stress is gone. Anxiety is gone. Conflict is gone. Expectations are gone. A new awareness arises out of the ashes. New priorities emerge. Necessities become clear and absurdities become evident in the power of RIGHT NOW.

FAITH RESPONSE:

_____

_____

_____

_____

_____

DAY 13

"Jesus saith unto him, 'Rise, take up your bed, and walk.'"
John 5:8

Every system is not healthy or just. Some systems require or even demand that we change them. Can you imagine for a moment the man at the Pool of Bethesda in the fifth chapter of John's Gospel, along with the other injured, impotent and helpless souls, just hanging around waiting for the "moving of the water"? And then when the healing waters are stirred, ONLY the first person to enter the water would be healed. Okay, whose idea was this? This man had been around the pool for thirty-eight years with decades of excuses and entrenched pathologies, and Jesus shows up and changes the system with the power of His words: "Rise, take up thy bed, and walk." The only way people change is when a system changes because people are connected to systems. Unjust systems need to change. Summons the courage for change and be the change.

FAITH RESPONSE:

_____

_____

_____

_____

_____

DAY 14

> *"Behold, I will do a new thing . . ."*
> **Isaiah 43:19a**

If you want something different, do something different. The human species are creatures of habit. Behavioral patterns are necessary for our survival, and repetition is the critical key to our cognitive, chemical, and physical processes. Just think for a moment how we would go through a day without learned habits and behavioral patterns. We could not speak, walk, think, drive a car, write, ad infinitum. Transitioning to a new level in your life will require you to do something new, something different. Start a new pattern of thought, a new muscle memory, or a new chemical reaction within your body. NEW. I know that word may be scary, but here's the alternative: if you don't do anything new, nothing is gained.

FAITH RESPONSE:

_____

_____

_____

_____

_____

_____

DAY 15

"For which of you, intending to build a tower, sitteth not down first, and counteth the cost, whether he have sufficient to finish it?"
Luke 14:28

A sustained effort and proper planning will lead to victory, so NEVER GIVE UP. Perhaps we began an endeavor or project and underestimated our resources—human and financial—and still came up short. Jesus says before one begins the undertaking of a construction project, one should count the cost. Many dreams evaporate and fail simply because our accounting was off. When you lay the groundwork of a vision, a plan, or a business proposal, spend adequate resources (spiritual, financial, physical, and organizational) at all these levels and never give up until you reach your goal. In fact, you can't give up because when you're weak, you'll be strengthened; when you're exhausted, a second wind will come; when money runs out, a new stream of income will find its way to you. NEVER GIVE UP!

FAITH RESPONSE:

_____

_____

_____

_____

DAY 16

"... now it shall spring forth ..."
Isaiah 43:19a

What God has planned for you is better than what you asked for so be patient. Most of us are prone to anxiety, restlessness, and even depression when our prayers seem unanswered. Just below the surface of our faith is a nervous palpitation of energy that can cause us to react suddenly or engage in language or thoughts that invalidate our prayers. My grandmother would say we were acting like an old cow. We can give a good pail of milk but turn around and kick it over. Isaiah says to the nation of Israel in chapter 43 "Behold, I will do a new thing; now it shall spring forth ..." I think most of us miss that small bud pushing through the soil of our faith because we want to see the full manifestation of our prayer, but look again. Can't you see it springing up?

FAITH RESPONSE:

_____

_____

_____

_____

_____

DAY 17

"Whatsoever ye shall bind on earth shall be bound in heaven."
Matthew 18:18

Conflicting desires is at the core of why we don't achieve many of our goals. When there is agreement, anything is possible. When Jesus speaks these words in Matthew 18:19 "If two of you shall agree on earth as touching any thing that they ask, it shall be done . . ." there is a natural and logical tendency to think in terms of a number of persons being together in agreement. I believe in the power of corporate prayer and even in the power of agreement, but what if Jesus had something much simpler in mind? We are created in three distinct components: body, mind and spirit. We can often times say one thing and mean another, and then do another. GUILTY. What if the implication Jesus makes is to get all of our "selves" TOGETHER and what we say YES to on earth will be echoed in eternity? Yes, completely Yes.

FAITH RESPONSE:

_____

_____

_____

_____

_____

DAY 18

"Count it all joy when you go through divers temptations . . ."
James 1:2a

Growth hurts, but I'll give God glory as I GROW through it. The early church was enduring more growing pains. The epistle of James was written to fortify the faith of the early believers facing strong opposition and fierce adversaries. This was the testing ground of their faith. James encourages the early church to grow through their adversities. They were surely going to go through them, but why not add some value to the experience. Grow through it. Every trial we face, every enemy we confront, every hardship we endure, every battle we fight are grounds for growth. We can make a decision to become stronger, smarter, wiser, and better through ALL of our trials. Don't just go through it and come out with nothing more than battle scars and a bitter spirit. Grow through it and evolve into the mature, faith-filled believer than can testify "I am a survivor!"

FAITH RESPONSE:

_____

_____

_____

_____

_____

DAY 19

"Every man's work shall be made manifest...it shall be revealed by fire..."
1 Corinthians 3:13

God is not obligated to cover you if He did not call you. I grew up hearing elder preachers say, "Some God sent and some just went." When I sensed a calling into ministry and kingdom service, I wanted to be certain and assured God was calling me to this work called ministry. God did not promise me I would never experience failure or that I would even be successful. The promise was "I'll be with you," and God has honored that covenant. There have been days when all I had was God, and I kept holding on to the promise of God's presence. Ministry offers so much more today than it did over thirty years ago when I acknowledged my call. Large churches, attractive packages, big budgets, and great locations are nice, but to be successful in ministry requires much more than these things. Every preacher and congregation will be tried in the fire and you will need the fireproof hand of God to cover you.

FAITH RESPONSE:

_____

_____

_____

_____

DAY 20

". . . the Lord gave, and the Lord hath taken away; blessed be the name of the Lord."
Job 1:21

Sometimes God's blessings are not in what is given, but in what is taken away. Job came to this realization after having lost all that he had and then stricken with disease. "The Lord giveth and the Lord taketh away; blessed be the name of the Lord." I am to bless the name of the Lord in the giving of the blessing, yes! In the receiving of the blessing, yes! I am also required to bless the name of the Lord in the taking away of a blessing? Huh? Wait a minute. I am to rejoice in the loss of a loved one, the loss of a child, the loss of health, the loss of a home, the loss of strength, the loss of money, the loss of a job? I'll be honest, that doesn't hint of any elements of joy bubbling inside of me, but it does speak of a grown-up faith in a timeless God. In time and throughout time, whatever God takes away God multiplies it and weaves it back into the fabric of our lives.

FAITH RESPONSE:

_____

_____

_____

_____

_____

DAY 21

"Casting all your care upon him, for he careth for you."
1 Peter 5:7

This problem is too big for me, but it's just the right size for God. I have often felt overwhelmed by challenges, problems, and projects that are supersized. At first glance my initial impression is I can handle this. With closer examination I wonder How in the world did I get into this? Just knowing I can put it all in the hands of an able God is immediately relieving and comforting. Whatever it is, large or small, put it all in His hands. God can handle it and He'll give you a strategy for a victorious outcome.

FAITH RESPONSE:

_____

_____

_____

_____

_____

_____

_____

_____

DAY 22

"Draw nigh to God, and he will draw nigh to you."
James 4:8a

Prayer is spending quality time with God. The reason I make a habit of spending time with God is so that when I get in trouble I don't have to introduce myself to Him. Stay close. Draw nigh unto God and He will draw nigh to you.

FAITH RESPONSE:

_____
_____
_____
_____
_____
_____
_____
_____
_____
_____
_____
_____

DAY 23

"Knowing this, that the trying of your faith worth patience."
James 1:3

The promises of God manifest in the fullness of time. God has not forgotten you. Waiting is one of the hardest things any of us can be asked to do, but if we with patience wait, we move from revelation to realization in God's time, with God's blessing, in God's Power. And God makes it worth the wait.

FAITH RESPONSE:

_____

_____

_____

_____

_____

_____

_____

_____

_____

_____

DAY 24

"But when the Comforter is come, whom I will send unto you from the Father, even the Spirit of truth, which proceeded from the father, he shall testify of me . . ."
John 15:26

In ANY situation you can be comfortable because you know the Comforter. The promise of our Christ is that He would send a Comforter to be with us. Life's noise can leave us agitated, disconnected, confused, and fearful. No matter where you are or what you are facing, you can find your anchoring center with the invitation of the Comforter to come.

FAITH RESPONSE:

_____

_____

_____

_____

_____

_____

_____

_____

DAY 25

"Christ hath redeemed us from the curse of the law, being made a curse for us..."
Galatians 3:13a

Because of the work of Christ, I am debt free. He paid the debt I owed. My record is expunged.

#I'm free
#MeToo
#DeliveredAgain
#LiftHimUP
#Balance -0-
#JesusPaidItAll

FAITH RESPONSE:

_____

_____

_____

_____

_____

_____

DAY 26

"Before I formed thee in the belly I knew thee..."
Jeremiah 1:5a

God chose me. In spite of my wounds and weaknesses, my faults and failures. God chose me. In fact, before there was a when or where, a here or there, God selected me. God has a holy habit of picking "nobodies" and making them "somebodies" without consulting anybody. This is God's way of demonstrating to us that He is in complete control. You were divinely selected. Before you chose God, God chose you. Every day from this day forward I will be reminded that God knew exactly who I was and who I would be when He chose me. In this moment I will simply say "THANK YOU." Dear Lord, on the days when I feel completely unworthy and undeserving of your grace and goodness, gently remind me of your preexisting knowledge of the purpose and plan for my life. It is your desire to mold me into the image you have of me. I surrender (Ephesians 1:11).

FAITH RESPONSE:
_____
_____
_____
_____
_____

DAY 27

"But we have this treasure in earthen vessels, that the excellency of the power may be of God, and not of us."
2 Corinthians 4:7

There is something beautiful and valuable in each of us. There are negative and inaccurate messages we have replaying in our head saying You're not good enough or You'll never amount to anything. Those messages are wrong. Hit the delete button, drag those messages to the mental trash can and forget them. What others have said about us and what we have said about ourselves is not what God has in mind. Embrace the mind of God. Say what He said, and we will be in the perfect will of God.

Dear God, deliver me from people who cannot see anything good in me. Deliver me from myself. Deliver me from reaffirming negative messages and inaccurate characterizations of who I am. You have placed a valuable treasure inside of me and I will keep digging until it is uncovered. You are the God who gives beauty for ashes. Help me reclaim my beauty and value.

FAITH RESPONSE:
_____
_____
_____
_____

DAY 28

"And the rest, some on boards, and some on broken pieces of the ship. And so it came to pass, that they escaped all safe to land."
Acts 27:44

As you cling to broken pieces, it seems as if you are slowly drifting toward the shoreline. Broken dreams, a broken heart, and broken promises have all left you adrift. The miracle is all of these experiences are floating devices bringing you closer to the shore. They were small fragments with enough buoyancy to keep you afloat. That's a miracle. Think about it. There was enough in the fragments of your life to sustain you. Don't dare think about going under now. Gather the fragments of your faith and bind them together with a memory of God's past provision and deliverance and watch God do it again!

Dear Lord, my survival has been a miraculous demonstration of your power. While others have been consumed, you have sustained my life. Deliver me again. Amen.

FAITH RESPONSE:

_____

_____

_____

_____

_____

DAY 29

"And she said, thine handmaid hath not any thing in the house, save a pot of oil."
2 Kings 4:2b

Life can sometimes hit us hard. So hard, we are left dazed and bewildered, asking questions like "If God is real and if God is with me, why is this happening to me?" A crisis has a way of narrowing our perspective and shaking our faith. We cannot manage what happens to us but we can measure how we respond. Even though we may not have much, we have something that will be the seed for our turnaround. Although you feel empty and broken, you still have something left and that is the something God will use to restore what you've lost. Whatever you have left, God can work with it. O God, help me to see what I cannot see, hear what I cannot hear, and give me the power to do what I can do. Amen.

FAITH RESPONSE:
_____
_____
_____
_____
_____
_____

DAY 30

"And he said, Lay not thine hand upon the lad, neither do thou anything unto him: for now I know that thou fearest God, seeing thou hast not withheld thy son, thine only son from me.
Genesis 22:12

God has perfect timing. Many of my prayers began this way, "Hurry Up, God!" A heart filled with anxiety and a trembling voice pumped doubt and disbelief coursing through my faith system. In my troubled mind, any delay would be a disaster. It was too much pressure on my prayer life, so I decided I will let God be God. I have some equity in my relationship with God and so do you. I lived through some things I thought would be my end. I felt some things I thought would cause me to implode. I endured some things I thought no other could endure, and I survived. In the midst of my inner turmoil, I was secured by a sense of peace and contentment, and that's when God showed up. Perfectly, inexplicably, and completely ON TIME. I've seen God work in time and on time. Let God work.

Dear Lord, You never announce the end of your plan at the beginning of your plan. I trust you. Amen.

FAITH RESPONSE:

_____

_____

_____

DAY 31

"When she had heard of Jesus, came in the press behind, and touched his garment."
Mark 5:27

The only power the enemy has over us is secrecy. There is an African proverb which says: "A concealed wound cannot be healed." Most of us suffer in silence and isolation because of shame. Rather than risk exposing a weakness, we'll suffer silently. No one knows we are wounded and hemorrhaging internally slowly losing strength and life. The woman who was afflicted with an issue of blood was a silent sufferer but she said to herself, "I don't have to touch Him, I only need to touch His hem." With one touch she discovers a hospital in the hem of His garment. This is one healing event in scripture when Jesus did not initiate healing. The wounded woman touched Him! Don't allow your pain to silence your voice or prevent you from being proactive concerning your healing. Give it to God and let your healing begin.

#METOO

FAITH RESPONSE:

_____

_____

_____

_____

DAY 32

"... Write the vision, and make it plain upon tables, that he may run that readeth it ... though it tarry, wait for it; because it will surely come."
Habakkuk 2:2-3

At the close of 2017, my daughter and I called a vision meeting. We sat down with a dry erase board and markers to write on our vision board. We were serious about what we wanted God to do for us and through us in 2018. Vision gives us divine direction. Habakkuk encourages us to write our vision clearly and place it where we can see it. Vision allows us to see it before we see it. With vision there is a component of faith; a faith that is connected to a solid spiritual life. If it seems slow in coming, don't get nervous. Just wait. It's on the way, and it will come at exactly the right time.

#20/20Vision

FAITH RESPONSE:
_____
_____
_____
_____
_____
_____

DAY 33

"In the world ye shall have tribulation but be of good cheer: I have overcome the world."
John 16:33b

We spend most of our time trying to avoid pain and suffering. We will use every available resource to evade difficult situations. The absence of pain and suffering—heartbreaks and heartaches, difficulties and setbacks—is unrealistic. The apostle Paul clearly notes "all things work together for the good . . ." (Romans 8:28) Although all things may not be good they have been determined to work for your good. And if it's not good yet, God is not finished.

Growing up as a young girl, I spent many of my summers in my mother's hometown of Cheraw, SC. My maternal grandmother, now deceased, corralled city children in her home for several weeks at a time. One of my more striking memories is my grandmother's fear of storms. As a storm drew near, she would come onto the front porch and call us inside because dark clouds were gathering. We crawled from under the house, climbed out of the ditch, and laid our bicycles on the edge of the dirt road at the urgency of her call. We had work to do. We had to cover every mirror in the house with sheets. The television and all lights were turned off, and there were no telephone calls going out or coming in because everyone in town was on storm watch. Finally, we had to get in bed and be quiet. We knew the routine.

With the first crashing of thunder she would reverently remind us, "Be quiet, God is talking." As I laid in the dark, quiet room in bed with all of the other children, my mind pondered her words, "God was talking in the storm." I easily agreed if God could speak to Elijah in an earthquake, a whirlwind or a still, small voice, God could also speak in a storm.

I'm a mother with my own child now and strangely enough, whenever a storm arises, my daughter will find her way to my room and get in my bed. There is something immensely comforting to her in my presence during a storm. When we are faced with one of life's storms, there is a place, a comforting place we can go. It is in the presence of the Lord. The psalmist declares "God is our refuge and strength, a very present help in trouble" (Psalm 46:1). So the very next time a storm hits—a storm in your marriage, a storm on your job, or in your church—remember SShhhhh ... God is talking.

#Listen

FAITH RESPONSE:

_____

_____

_____

_____

_____

_____

_____

_____

DAY 34

"Finally, bretheren, whatsoever things are true, whatsoever things are honest, whatsoever things are just, whatsoever things are pure, whatsoever things are lovely, whatsoever things are of good report; if there be any virtue, and if there be any praise, think on these things."
Philippians 4:8

There is a sign on my mirror by Elsie de Wolfe that I read every morning. It says: "I'm going to make everything around me beautiful - that will be my life." People can act so ugly. They think ugly thoughts, say ugly words, and do ugly things. Imagine if we would think something beautiful what a lovely world this would be. We spend most of our lives searching for the beautiful when we have been given the power and ability to create something beautiful, grow something beautiful, be a part of something beautiful. With so much ugliness in the world and in our lives, begin each day with something beautiful. A spoken blessing for your enemy. A kind thought toward your betrayer. Time shared with one of our elders. Assistance to your neighbor. The apostle Paul says, "whatsoever things are lovely . . . think on these things." Just think.

FAITH RESPONSE:

_____

_____

_____

DAY 35

"When I was a child, I spake as a child, I understood as a child, I thought as a child: but when I became a man, I put away childish things."
1 Corinthians 13:11

When I was a child I did childish things. Now that I am older, sometimes I just have a bad day. One crazy idea; one decision I didn't completely think through; one impulsive reaction and it's a bad day. We are not exempt from having a bad day, a weak moment, or a temporary cognitive processing disorder. It's just one bad day. Whether it's a good day or a bad day, GOD IS FAITHFUL. God is faithful to review our faults and through his Son, Jesus, count us faultless. All of my days fall under the faithful hand of a forgiving God. That makes any bad day so much better.

FAITH RESPONSE:
_____
_____
_____
_____
_____
_____
_____

DAY 36

"Know ye not that they which run in a race run all, but one receiveth the prize? So run, that ye may obtain."
1 Corinthians 9:24

Lance Armstrong, a world class athlete, was preparing to compete in an upcoming Tour de France biking marathon. He was the natural favorite to win #7. He won his previous six races. Between race six and seven, he was diagnosed with testicular cancer. Doctors did not expect him to survive. Not only did he survive, he came back to win his seventh consecutive victory. When a reporter asked him how he prepared for his seventh race after battling cancer, his response was "I prepared for race #7 like all the other races. First, I decide to win. Second, I train to win."DECIDE to win and then TRAIN to win. Most of us are defeated before we ever begin because we have not made the decision to win. Deciding to win is half the battle. We must then TRAIN to win. That's what the apostle Paul was teaching the Church at Corinth (1 Corinthians 9:24-27). In order to win the race of the Christian journey, we must train like an athlete for a marathon race. However, there is one distinct difference. EVERYONE wins if you cross the finish line. And the prize? Eternal rewards!

FAITH RESPONSE:
_____
_____
_____

DAY 37

> *"Delight thyself also in the Lord; and he shall give thee the desires of thine heart."*
> **Psalm 37:4**

Sanctification is the process by and through which the Holy Spirit stimulates us to stop wanting the things we want to satisfy our flesh or our ego and begin to desire the things God wants for us. This is exactly what the Psalmist David means in Psalm 37:4. When the Holy Spirt resides in us we will begin to desire the things of God. When we desire the things of God we receive them. We all have plans, dreams, and goals, and most of us want God to endorse our plan for our lives. Full Stop. The believer must go through the process of sanctification in order to ensure there is no confusion concerning whose will wins out in the end. Can I give you a hint? It will not be yours or mine. God will bend us, break us, mold us, and shape us until our will is lost in His will.

FAITH RESPONSE:

_____

_____

_____

_____

_____

DAY 38

"And when Paul had gathered a bundle of sticks, and laid them on the fire, there came a viper out of the heat, and fastened on his hand."
Acts 28:3

Surviving a shipwreck should have qualified Paul for any reality television show or miniseries. The ship was completely destroyed. Paul, however, along with crew members, survived by clinging to broken pieces of the ship. Now on a strange island among strange people, the natives gave shelter and provision to the storm-ravished men. While gathering wood for a fire, a snake bites Paul on the hand. The natives thought surely Paul would meet his end after being bitten by a venomous snake. Paul had the presence of mind to shake the snake off. They waited for him to die but no harm came to him. Shaking off snakes becomes part of the incredible survival skills for the apostle. I would suggest you learn the skill. Snakes come out of hidden places when you least expect them and sometimes in your most vulnerable moments. For the next leg of your Christian journey, shaking off snakes is a "must have" in your skill set. Shake them off and live through it.

FAITH RESPONSE:
_____
_____
_____

DAY 39

". . . Master, carest thou not that we perish?"
Mark 3:38

In a panic, any of us are subject to have wild, wild, wild thoughts. This question from the disciples of Jesus in the midst of a storm when they think the ship is about to go underwater is an obvious moment of crisis. Their thoughts have gone wild. Master, do you care? Do you care that I am overwhelmed and stressed out and there is no relief in sight? Do you care that I've lost my job and no new employment is on the horizon? Master, do you care that I have been mistreated and disgraced? What the disciples failed to realize in that moment when the storm was most intense was Jesus was on board the ship. He was not in the mountains praying or on the shoreline teaching. HE WAS IN THE BOAT. It wasn't the storm that awakened him, it was their cry out for help. He's right there. Cry out for help and watch God demonstrate how much He cares for you. He cares enough to leave His presence with you.

FAITH RESPONSE:

_____

_____

_____

_____

_____

DAY 40

"Yea, though I walk through the valley of the shadow of death, I will fear no evil: for thou art with me; thy rod and thy staff they comfort me."
Psalm 23:4

Whenever I find myself in a difficult place I revisit a book I read years ago by Iyanla Vanzant entitled *Value in the Valley*. She subscribes to the notion that the darkest and most difficult places of our lives offer us great treasures. It changed my perspective on my valley experiences. Any challenging period in our lives has within it the possibility of producing treasures like patience, perseverance, strength, ingenuity, creativity, determination, flexibility, and a grateful spirit. No one falls in love with a valley experience. No one enjoys navigating among the shadows and from the lowest places. In the valley we become painfully aware of our humanness and limitations. The light of the mountain top is where we would prefer to be, but we only reach those heights by traversing through the valley. In the valley all we have is God, and God is all we need.

FAITH RESPONSE:
_____
_____
_____
_____

DAY 41

"One thing that I desire and that will I seek after..."
Psalm 27:4

In the age of multitasking, I've reached the age of focusing my attention on one thing. Time has a wonderful, sensible wisdom. The juggling act of multitasking left me filled with anxiety and incomplete projects. Women quite naturally do more than one thing at a time, but this new age multitasking made me feel less than a supermom and more like a nervous Neanderthal. David's wisdom reminds us that we can experience the fullness of God's presence by focusing on ONE THING—God. When we make God our priority and serve with laser focus, God will make all things clear.

Dear Lord, as you give me one day at a time, give me the strength and ability to accomplish one task at a time and eventually everything will be complete, including me. Amen.

FAITH RESPONSE:

_____

_____

_____

_____

_____

_____

DAY 42

"And Jesus being full of the Holy Ghost returned from Jordan, and was led by the Spirit into the wilderness . . ."
Luke 4:1

Here is the strategy of the enemy to defeat us. First, our enemy sends the test of our strength. Second, our enemy sends the test of our weakness. With this highly classified information, our enemy will seek every opportunity to destroy us, destroy our character, our good name, our life goals and achievements. When your tests come, and they will come, remember the words of the apostle Paul: "In my weakness, then am I made strong" (2 Corinthians 12:9). When and where I am strong, I will appear as if I'm weak. It's a game of strategy we can win every single time. Jesus won in the wilderness. The surprise is God led Him into His wilderness. Where God leads, God sustains.

FAITH RESPONSE:
_____
_____
_____
_____
_____

DAY 43

"Hast not thou made an hedge about him, and about his house, and about all that he hath on every side?"
Job 1:10

God has so completely blessed your life it has confused the enemy. The enemy cannot get what he cannot see. God will put a hedge of protection around you and everything that belongs to you. Amen.

FAITH RESPONSE:

_____
_____
_____
_____
_____
_____
_____
_____
_____
_____

DAY 44

"Blessed are they which are persecuted for righteousness sake: for theirs is the kingdom of heaven."
Matthew 5:10

There are those in power who retain power by persecuting the weak. It makes them feel strong. Jesus said that those who are persecuted should rejoice. Really? Rejoicing in the face of persecution subverts the power of our oppressors. It robs them of a satisfaction drawn out of our fear. Jesus said be happy when you are persecuted because then you rob your persecutors and they themselves are weakened. So, be happy.

FAITH RESPONSE:

_____

_____

_____

_____

_____

_____

_____

_____

DAY 45

"You're a tree replanted in Eden, bearing fresh fruit every month, never dropping a leaf, always in blossom."
Psalm 1:3

Seasons come and seasons go. I must admit I wish I could live in a perpetual state of springtime. Everything fresh and new. Growth and vitality surrounding everything. Out of nowhere there appears a budding flower pushing up through the soil. However, seasons change. With every change of season there is a rebuilding, a shedding away, a death. All of these must be a part of the cycle of life. Through the harshest of winters there is unspeakable suffering. In the most vibrant days of summer there is a harvesting and an abundance. All of these must be. Through the many changes of our lives we come to an awareness of God as the sustainer of life. The psalmist declares when we anchor our lives in the Word of God, "You're a tree replanted in Eden, bearing fresh fruit every month, never dropping a leaf, always in blossom." No matter what season your life is in God says, You're always in blossom.

FAITH RESPONSE:

_____

_____

_____

_____

DAY 46

"... greater is he that is in you, than he that is in the world."
1 John 4:4

My philosophy on leadership is simple: be better than you think you can be. Throughout our lives, we live with old messages of inadequacy and we learned not to expect very much from ourselves. Average grades, a mediocre job and life was good enough to keep us from disgrace and applying ourselves with greater effort. Exceed your own expectations. Be unafraid to be greater and then plant seeds of greatness in others. This is the true embodiment of leadership.

FAITH RESPONSE:

_____

_____

_____

_____

_____

_____

_____

_____

_____

DAY 47

"... and his hand was restored whole as the other."
Luke 6:10b

At some point in each of our lives we will need to be restored. Perhaps a relationship, our finances, or our health will be ravished, and we will apply our faith in the direction of restoration. When we see others apply and model faith behavior, don't judge or criticize them. Simply support them. We only know what they've allowed us to see. On the outside looking in we see only limitation, selfishness, and lack ... until we know the whole story. Having the courage to stand after a debilitating illness is a testimony to one's faith in the God who completely restores. Bouncing back from devastating financial disaster or divorce is a triumphant act of courage. We can honor God with the broken pieces of our lives. Restoration is God's full-time business.

FAITH RESPONSE:

___

___

___

___

___

___

DAY 48

"I am the light of the world."
John 9:5b

In Ancient Greece, the runners in the marathon race were required to carry a lit torch the distance of the race. Through the winding roads and hills of the countryside, only the well-disciplined athlete could compete and win. Oddly enough, the winner was not the first to cross the finish line. Victory was given to the one who crossed the finish line WITH THEIR TORCH STILL LIT.

The opening of our contemporary Olympics reenact the lighting of the torch to commence the Olympic Games. In these games, athletes compete for medals, honors and endorsements—earthly prizes. The apostle Paul urges the Church at Corinth (1 Corinthians 9:24-27) to run for an eternal prize that far outweighs any wealth or glory we may receive on earth. The winds of life will blow. Our goal is to finish the race with our torch still lit. Here's my "every day of the year" resolution written by Henry Dixon Loes: This little light of mine, I'm going to let it shine. Let it shine, let it shine, let it shine.

FAITH RESPONSE:
_____
_____
_____

DAY 49

"The effectual fervent prayer of a righteous person availeth much."
James 5:16b

I have been on a pilgrimage of prayer over the last several months and have rediscovered the power and necessity of time spent in God's presence. Prayer time is a special grace of God for the weary traveler. Prayer helps one to recalculate the direction and destination one travels. The comforting time of prayer is the recognition and acceptance that we are not traveling alone. We have a fellow traveler and guide who goes with us up every steep hill, across every rocky road, through every dangerous passageway, and rests with us at every landing. The comforting presence of the Holy Spirit is with us on our journey. The Spirit's goal is not to make it easier, but to reveal to us the worthwhile nature of the trip, to track our progress, and inspire us to the end. It doesn't matter how long it takes for us to get there, as long as we get there.

FAITH RESPONSE:

_____

_____

_____

_____

_____

DAY 50

"Speaking to yourselves in psalms and Hymns and spiritual songs, singing and making melody in your heart to the Lord..."
Ephesians 5:19

The memory of some rough road in my life always returns me to the wonderful hymn writers whose lyrics gave me strength during some of my darkest hours. Deeply rooted in the African American Church tradition, the default setting for any crisis event has always been one of the hymns of the church. Now that I am older, they mean so much more to me. After revisiting one of my more painful experiences with a trusted friend, one of the songs of my survival surfaced: "What a fellowship, what a joy divine leaning on the Everlasting Arms." Have you ever had to lean on God? Weighted down with a situation so heavy you could not stand upright, you could only lean? There is no greater safety and security than in the able arms of God. No matter the weight of our problems or petitions, every day we can lean on the Everlasting Arms.

FAITH RESPONSE:

_____

_____

_____

_____

_____

DAY 51

"... they uncovered the roof where he was: and when they had broken it up, they let down the bed wherein the sick of the palsy lay."
Mark 2:4b

All of your life you've been trying to understand why you don't exactly fit in. Your family context, relationship with co-workers and colleagues, even within most of your social groups. It's difficult to explain but the awkwardness is evident at every family gathering or social event. The underlying message is "I just don't belong here." Perhaps I can explain your chronic agitation with one word: DIFFERENT. Every place we are born is not where we belong. Something greater calls us out. Something greater sets us apart. It doesn't make us better than someone else, just different. We don't know why we have been selected, we just are. Most people in our circle of familiarity will never understand because they are still negotiating the reasons THEY were not the chosen one. Being different requires a different set of friends, a different mindset, a different context, a different perspective, but most importantly, a different kind of faith. BE DIFFERENT.

FAITH RESPONSE:

_____

_____

_____

_____

DAY 52

"... you are of more value than many sparrows."
Matthew 10:31b

With a broken wing, it's hard to fly and hard to sing. With a broken wing, our heights are lowered, and our sight is limited. A broken wing is a part of each of our stories. In some cases, a special grace of God comes to heal our brokenness in order to regain strength to fly again. It is in the helping and in the healing our brokenness is mended. The very special grace of God is when two who are broken find each other, heal each other, and help each other to fly again and fly higher. This is the sum total of God's amazing grace that makes us sing.

FAITH RESPONSE:

___

___

___

___

___

___

___

DAY 53

"In the year that King Uzziah died I saw also the Lord..."
Isaiah 6:1a

Significant events that have taken place in our life are marked by memory. We remember exactly where we were and what we were doing. One of the biblical benchmark examples is in the year of the nation of Israel's national mourning, the prophet Isaiah marks his conversion experience. King Uzziah died and Isaiah claimed it was then that "I saw the Lord." God wants to radically change your life as he did with Isaiah, but you have to SEE HIM. This begs the question, What's obscuring your vision? What is preventing you from seeing the full majesty and glory of God at work in your life and the world? With a daily schedule crammed with meetings, greetings, family responsibilities, work obligations, and so much more, it will take only one majestic encounter with the ETERNAL to bring your life's work and mission into focus. Just ONE.

Dear Lord, help us to see you more clearly and follow you more nearly each day. Amen.

FAITH RESPONSE:

_____

_____

_____

_____

DAY 54

"The steps of a good person are ordered by the Lord."
Psalm 37:23a

My vehicle has one of the top-line navigation systems. I press a button, convey my destination to the operator, directions are downloaded to my vehicle, and I'm on my way. Growing up as a young girl, that is not how we traveled. My father was trained in the military and he knew how to read a map. Whenever we planned a family vacation, my dad would purchase a map, study it, and chart out his driving route. We always arrived at our destination. Reading a map is a lost art. With so many modern conveniences at the touch of our fingers, we easily forget there was a time when we had no access to technology. The Bible has long been a roadmap for my life and for so many others. Pick it up, study it, chart out the travel route, and you will always arrive at your desired destination. Sometimes broken, sometimes bruised, sometimes tired, but you will arrive.

FAITH RESPONSE:

_____

_____

_____

_____

_____

DAY 55

"The Lord is my shepherd, I shall not want."
Psalm 23:1

The Lord is my Shepherd, and I LACK NOTHING. What a word to lean on and lift us. The twenty-third Psalm is a timeless word for any and every season of our life. I LACK NOTHING because the Lord is my Shepherd. When we become fully aware of God's ability to provide everything we need, He truly becomes our Shepherd. We experience God as a constant presence and a capable provider.

FAITH RESPONSE:

_____

_____

_____

_____

_____

_____

_____

_____

DAY 56

"Surely goodness and mercy shall follow me all the days of my life . . ."
Psalm 23:6a

What a blessed promise from God. All the days ahead of you will be blessed because of what Dr. Charles E. Booth calls "The Inseparable Twins." Can you imagine having goodness and mercy in tow wherever you go? Now you understand why people give you the side eye and whisper underneath their breath as you pass by. You are completely flanked by divine company and divine favor. It does not matter the voice of the enemy that tries to shake your faith and cause you anxiety. God has not brought you this far to abandon you. His plan for your life is lasting joy and success ALL THE DAYS OF YOUR LIFE (John 15:16). Live long and live well.

FAITH RESPONSE:

_____

_____

_____

_____

_____

DAY 57

"Teach me, O Lord, the ways of thy statutes; and I shall keep it unto the end. Give me understanding, and I shall keep thy law; yea, I shall observe them with my whole heart."
Psalm 119:33-34

All of us should have some guiding principles that support core values in our life. The psalmist clearly uses the Word of God as the guiding principles for his life and petitions God to be the teacher and he the student. Further, there is a commitment on the part of the student that what he or she learns will be applied to one's life, totally and completely. There is no better thing to ask God for than understanding. The scriptures remind us "in all thy getting, get understanding" (Proverbs 4:7b). To understand is to have a full revelation and application of God's Word. To have full revelation we must study and perform the Word. Incidentally, we have the best teacher in the Universe.

FAITH RESPONSE:

_____

_____

_____

_____

_____

DAY 58

"Know ye not that your body is the temple of the Holy Ghost . . ."
1 Corinthians 6:19a

I have made a conscious decision to bow in humble submission to holy hormones. Midlife brings a different set of challenges to womanhood: madness, mystery, and misery. The reverence of your temple is what makes those wonderful biological chemicals firing and misfiring throughout your system achieve balance. We honor our temple during this sacred season with a balance of rest, good nutritional habits, exercise, and plenty of laughter. Let your hair down and laugh at yourself and your sister friends who join you on this journey.

Dear Lord, help me to surrender the things of my youth and embrace the wisdom and grace of my years. You are my soul's anchor during my internal storms. Let me hear your voice gently speak "Peace Be Still." Amen.

FAITH RESPONSE:

_____

_____

_____

_____

_____

DAY 59

". . . Be ye holy; for I am holy."
1 Peter 1:16

What do you do with an unholy arrangement? Detangle.

Gracious and Merciful God, thank you for the power to forgive others and the power to forgive myself. Renew and restore my mind and strength that I may be in right relationship with you. Help me discern the good you have purposed for my life and avoid the soul ties that keep me from reaching the blessed place you have prepared for me. Thank you for your grace and goodness that remind me each day how valuable I am. Amen.

FAITH RESPONSE:

_____
_____
_____
_____
_____
_____
_____
_____

DAY 60

"Then Peter said, silver and gold have I none; but such as I have give I thee: In the name of Jesus Christ of Nazareth rise up and walk."
Acts 3:6

God will not do for you what you can do for yourself. It is a divine partnership when we invite God into our circumstance. We somehow have the expectation of simply naming it and claiming it and it will magically appear. We can do that until our lungs collapse and never realize God's best for our life. Until we do the work required to make our dream a reality and our vision come to fruition, we will only experience a small fraction of God's blessings. When we partner with God, wonderful things will begin to happen. God will use our voice to inspire and ignite others. God will use gifted and resourceful people through holy acquaintance to provide information and access to resources we need. God will open doors - all kinds of doors, to connect us with people and partners and necessary resources for the completion of our intended purpose. I'm all for decreeing and declaring and afterwards, I'M GETTING TO WORK!

FAITH RESPONSE:

_____

_____

_____

_____

DAY 61

"Go to the ant ... consider her ways, and be wise ... provideth her meat in the summer, and gathereth her food in the harvest."
Proverbs 6:6-8

We are so busy working on our self-worth, we've paid no attention to our net worth. We schedule our hair/make-up and nail appointments. We make time and money for the barbershop, the tailor, the Italian loafers. We have to look our best always, so we are headed to the next shopping event. I'm all for self-empowerment and self-improvement, but how many designer watches and purses do you really need? And shoes and suits and ties and accessories? Stop SHOPPING and start SAVING. That is the best self-empowerment and self-improvement you can gift yourself. When you see those bank numbers steadily increasing, a new pair of shoes becomes irrelevant. The ant is a wise insect. In the words of Jesus: Go and do likewise.

FAITH RESPONSE:

_____
_____
_____
_____
_____
_____

DAY 62

"... and he received them and spake unto them of the kingdom of God, and healed them that had need of healing."
Luke 9:11b

Self-care is equivalent to self-love. We can become so consumed with our caring, compassionate nature that we overlook giving "soul" care to ourselves. People and responsibilities pull us and drain our mental, emotional, physical, and psychic energy. When exactly are we to refuel and refit? Not often enough. This kind of stress eventually takes a toll on our mental and physical health. Jesus mentions the proverb "physician heal thyself" in Luke 4:23a. Even though he does not commend the advice, perhaps there is some wisdom in it we should follow. When you're tired, rest. When you're overworked, take a long weekend to recharge. When you're frustrated, talk it through with a trusted colleague or a professional. Self-care says I am important to me.

FAITH RESPONSE:

_____

_____

_____

_____

_____

_____

DAY 63

"And God is able to make all grace abound toward you; that ye, always having all sufficiency in all things, may abound to every good work."
2 Corinthians 9: 8

I experienced a breakthrough moment a few weeks ago when I understood what the apostle Paul was communicating to the Church at Corinth. He was encouraging them to become gracious givers because we serve a God who graciously gives to us. What God gives to us is more than a blessing. God adds grace to the blessing. In other words, it will last longer, go further, and accomplish more than you expected or were guaranteed. The blessing will lead to another blessing that will meet another need and every need will be met because there is total sufficiency in the blessings of God. God can make a little bit go a long way when our hearts are set to honor Him.

FAITH RESPONSE:
_____
_____
_____
_____
_____
_____

DAY 64

"And every man that striveth for the mastery is temperate in all things."
1 Corinthians 9:25a

Too much relaxation makes you lazy. Too much sleep makes you tired. Too much food makes you overweight. Too much work makes you a workaholic. Too much alcohol will make you a drunk. Too much of anything is not good for you. The words of the apostle Paul says when we master our appetites, feelings, and desires, we master our life.

#Balance
#NoSloppyLiving
#BeVigilant
#MindOverMatter

FAITH RESPONSE:

_____

_____

_____

_____

_____

_____

_____

DAY 65

"But I am like a green olive tree in the house of God..."
Psalm 52:1a

In Ancient Greece, the olive tree was a symbol of peace and friendship. In the sacred story of Noah in the book of Genesis, he releases a dove to determine if land was near after the cataclysmic flood. The dove returns with an olive branch; one of God's first signs of peace. To extend "an olive branch" to someone is to seek to reestablish peace and renew a friendship. David writes this psalm when King Saul was at odds with him. Saul's jealousy and insecurities were focused on destroying David when he makes this declaration: I want peace and friendship. It would be altogether lovely to have more people who were like "olive trees" in the House of God.

FAITH RESPONSE:

_____
_____
_____
_____
_____
_____
_____

DAY 66

"Neither do men light a candle and put it under a bushel, but on a candlestick..."
Matthew 5:15

Have you ever wondered why you never fit in? You are cut from a different cloth. My grandmother was a seamstress and that is the expression of someone who knew fabric and material, textiles and texture. You are cut from a different cloth. We are children of the Light and wherever we go, we glow. Can't hide it. Can't explain it. Can't deny it. No apologies necessary. We glow. If there is someone in your context that cannot handle your glow, they will always seek a way to diminish your shine. The God in you is not meant to be kept a secret. Go public with your praise. Go public with you witness. Go public with your service and shine. There's a light in you and you were made to shine. You have been called "out of darkness into his marvelous light" (Peter 2:9b).

FAITH RESPONSE:

_____

_____

_____

_____

_____

_____

DAY 67

"Let us therefore come boldly unto the throne of grace, that we may obtain mercy, and find grace in the time of need."
Hebrews 4:16

No one understands what you need better than God. We have a God who is in touch with our reality and who understands our humanity. We have a God who can relate to our issues, knows our struggles, and understands our idiosyncrasies. No problem is too big, no trial too great, no temptation too strong, no burden too heavy, no sin too shameful, no circumstance too difficult, no life too messed up. We can come boldly to the throne of grace. Here's what we'll find when we get there: grace, mercy, and help in our time of need. That's what I need.

FAITH RESPONSE:

_____
_____
_____
_____
_____
_____
_____

DAY 68

"Now after the death of Moses the servant of the Lord it came to pass, that the Lord speaks unto Joshua, the son of Nun..."
Joshua 1:1

The biggest issue the nation of Israel had to face as they emerged from Egyptian bondage was not the challenge of giants in the land of Canaan, it was the challenge of CHANGE. They just could not get over the death of Moses. The paralyzing nature of their grief and resistance to change left them in the plains of Moab lamenting the loss of Moses for weeks. When God decides to make a change, it does not matter whether or not we agree. God's sovereign right to change will happen whether we like it or not. When we fail to agree with God's plan, including ALL the change orders, we impede our own progress and delay the victories and blessings ahead for us. When God speaks, simply say AMEN, so let it be.

FAITH RESPONSE:

_____

_____

_____

_____

_____

_____

DAY 69

"And I will give thee the treasures of darkness, and hidden riches of secret places, that thou mayest know that I, the Lord, which call thee by thy name, am the God of Israel."
Isaiah 45:3

God says I'll lead you to hidden treasure in secret places. What a promise! So, here's the prayer.

Dear Lord, every good and perfect gift comes from you. You are the source of my provision and abundance. I humbly ask you to lead me and guide me along the path and direction I should go. Fill my cup until it overflows, and my life gives testimony that you are the God who knows me by my name. Amen.

FAITH RESPONSE:

_____

_____

_____

_____

_____

_____

_____

_____

DAY 70

"... Lo, I see four men loose, walking in the midst of the fire, and they have no hurt; and the form of the fourth is like the Son of God."
Daniel 3:25

Only our God could pull off a miracle like this. Shadrach, Meshach, and Abednego put their trust in God to deliver them from the King's fiery furnace. They refused to bow to the golden image of other gods. With a conviction as hot as the fire itself, they put their life on the line and the God of their deliverance met them in the fire. What a strange place to meet God. In the fire. God will often allow us to experience "hot" situations only to remind us we are never without HIS presence. The next time life has you "fired up" and it becomes hot and uncomfortable, remember the abiding presence of God is with you. Don't be afraid. Faith is forged in the fires of life and only God can pull off a rescue from the fire and you come out not even smelling like smoke.

FAITH RESPONSE:

_____

_____

_____

_____

_____

DAY 71

"Sit ye here, while I shall pray."
Mark 14:32b

If anyone had the authority to speak on managing stress, it was our Savior. Perhaps we can utilize his successful strategies for overcoming stressful periods in our life.

1) *Pause.* Jesus always found a place of withdrawal and rest. Our over scheduled lives can leave us depleted. Find time to recharge and refresh yourself.
2) *People.* Jesus took Peter, James, and John with him on his retreat from the multitudes. All of us need support if we are to survive stressful times. We need others to assist us.
3) *Prayer.* Jesus fell on the ground and prayed. Stress can weigh you down and have you on the verge of collapse. Take your burdens to the Lord and leave them there.
4) *Press.* Jesus arises from His place of prayer to press through, for His betrayer was at hand. We can deal directly with the issues that stress us out rather than running away from them or ignoring them altogether.

Consider the way in which Jesus dealt with his stressful moment and you can be relieved of your anxiety and worry. Just leave it all in God's hands.

FAITH RESPONSE:

_____

_____

_____

_____

DAY 72

"But it is good for me to draw near to God: I have put my trust in the Lord, that I may declare all thy works."
Psalm 73:28

Answers aren't always what we need. Sometimes all we need is clarity. We simply need God's power and presence to help us live with unanswered questions. Asaph wanted justice for the righteous. Let's be honest, we all have sung this song before. Why do the wicked prosper and the righteous are left languishing? Why does it come easy for the wicked and the righteous have to struggle? It just doesn't seem fair. That's what Asaph said when he looked around. When he looked within the pain was overwhelming. Life just didn't make sense and he didn't get clarity until he went into the sanctuary of God. In that holy space, Asaph was able to look ahead and see the outcome of the wicked. Asaph could see a day coming when God will be the great equalizer and settle every account. You can only see THAT day when you look up. Keep looking UP!

FAITH RESPONSE:

_____

_____

_____

_____

_____

DAY 73

"... they laughed us to scorn, and despised us..."
Nehemiah 2:19

I'm sure you've had to deal with discouragement before because it is a useful tool of the enemy. It is difficult to keep your spirits up when others are looking and laughing and making critical comments. That is exactly what Nehemiah had to face when he accepts the assignment to rebuild the wall around Jerusalem. He offers us some helpful hints on how to handle our critics. Don't stop working on your vision. Respond to your critics with prayer. When criticism increases against you, increase your prayer life. Time spent dealing with enemies is time spent away from our purpose and assignment. They are not worth that kind of attention. God can handle your haters. Nehemiah does more than just pray, he does something practical. He sets up a watch. With a brick in one hand and a sword in the other, he and his willing workers are prepared to build and do battle at the same time. Nehemiah refuses to come down to the level of his enemies. #Don'tLetThemGetYouDown

FAITH RESPONSE:

_____

_____

_____

_____

DAY 74

"The blessing of the Lord, it maketh rich, and he addeth no sorrow with it."
Proverbs 10:22

Whenever I have to make a weighty decision I pay close attention to how I feel. The body has a wonderful wisdom that communicates with the conscious mind. We may believe that accepting the job or relocating to another city or purchasing a new home is a blessing, and it may well be, but if you are anxious and losing sleep and fluctuating between decisions, it is adding sorrow. The writer of Proverbs says God's blessings are rich and they add no sorrow. In other words, the blessing does not become a burden, and if it does, perhaps it is not a blessing at all. If I make a decision and my body is feeling drained of energy or my mind is scrambled when I think of it, that is my signal to rethink my decision. When God blesses us, God makes our lives rich. The blessing causes us to smile. The blessing makes us rest well at night. Anything less than that is a caution sign.
#STAYWOKE

FAITH RESPONSE:

_____

_____

_____

_____

DAY 75

"... put thou my tears in thy bottle ..."
Psalm 56:8

I have a smartphone that's very smart. It keeps track of my fitness and activity by recording the number of steps I take every day. Technology is amazing. We also have an AMAZING GOD—a God who notices our tears, keeps track of our tears, is touched by our tears, and remembers our tears. David wrote these words while in the custody of his enemies. It was a scary and difficult time. David was wondering if he would survive capture. Overwhelmed by the prospect, he prays, "Put my tears in a bottle."

Have you ever felt incapacitated by a problem and you had no words to speak, only tears? Well, every tear matters to God and tears are prayers too. Don't cry all of your faith away. Be assured God keeps track of our tears like an accountant with a ledger. No tear is wasted, no tear is overlooked.

Dear Lord, thank you for holding me close during difficult days. You are my comforter. Your Word reminds me, "They that sow in tears shall reap in joy" (Psalm 126:5).

FAITH RESPONSE:

_____

_____

_____

DAY 76

[forgive] "seventy times seven."
Matthew 18:22b

For Peter, this forgiveness thing was a bit much to swallow. He needed a reasonable number of forgiveness contracts and he may be able to get through this particular requirement. Peter inquires if seven is a fair number of forgiveness contracts to maintain. Jesus makes the point that there are no boundaries when it comes to forgiveness. Jesus then tells the parable of why we should forgive as opposed to how many times we should forgive. Luke 6:37 says "... forgive and you will be forgiven." All of us will need forgiveness at some point, so we are to forgive as many times as needed so that we may qualify for forgiveness.

FAITH RESPONSE:
_____
_____
_____
_____
_____
_____
_____

DAY 77

"For God hath not given us the spirit of fear; but of power, and of love, and of a sound mind."
2 Timothy 1:7

When the apostle Paul offers this counsel to young Pastor Timothy he was obviously afraid of something. Perhaps the assignment at the Church in Ephesus or insecure in his abilities to handle an "urban" church. We are clear that false teachers had cropped up in the church and they were causing serious problems. Paul reminds Timothy and us that our response to fear is never to allow it to paralyze or intimidate us. Fear is mental enslavement and often holds us captive based on what might happen in the future. We are afraid of what we don't know. Instead of responding out of our emotions, let's be sensible and steady. A sound mind dismisses fear. Be spiritual. Be strategic. Be secure in the Word and power of God. Fear is a thief that will rob you of the joy of living. Draw a line in the sand and say, "Not today or any other day." I will trust God with my days ahead and God will navigate me through every situation and storm. God will help you.

FAITH RESPONSE:

_____

_____

_____

_____

DAY 78

Bless the Lord, O my soul: and all that is within me, bless his holy name. Bless the Lord, O my soul, and forget not all his benefits: who forgiveth all thine iniquities; who healeth all thy diseases..."
Psalm 103:1-3

Counting the many blessings of God is good spiritual arithmetic. All of the sins God has forgiven and all of the healings we have experienced are in the long equation of God's power and ability active in our life. Just pause for a moment. Don't think about the many times God has delivered you; think about the last time God delivered you. Bless His Name! What about the last time God rescued you from an enemy's trap? Bless His Name! What about the last bad decision that could have cost you everything? Bless His Name! The blessings of God are so numerous they require us to be in a continual state of praise. God continues to forgive us and continues to heal us. God keeps doing great and wonderful things in our life.

FAITH RESPONSE:

_____
_____
_____
_____
_____

DAY 79

"When my father and mother forsake me, then the Lord will take me up."
Psalm 27:10

This must be the ultimate fear of one's life when the two people who should be there for you to support you are missing from your life. Absent by death or departure, they are absent. There is a staggering feeling of aloneness that saturates your soul. This is the time when a full evaluation must be made of all of your relationships. It is the time you must determine who stays in your life and who goes. Here are some clues: if they strengthen you, nourish your soul, and want to see you succeed, they are a keeper. If they drain you of your mental energy, require constant emotional maintenance, if they are hypersensitive, self-centered, and selfish, let them go. The psalmist declares when the needful relationships and support is not present, God will ALWAYS be there.

FAITH RESPONSE:

_____

_____

_____

_____

_____

DAY 80

"And Peter followed afar off."
Luke 22:54b

Peter's self-confident comment to follow Jesus to prison and even to death blows up in this one moment. His failure was following Jesus from a distance. Peter had the privilege of walking closely with Jesus for nearly three years; enjoying the benefits of this popular, charismatic miracle worker. For fear that he would be discovered as a follower of Jesus and arrested himself, Peter determines not to disown Jesus, but follow him from a distance. Close, but not connected. In the vicinity but certainly not near. We gradually fall further away from God when we follow from afar. We don't need signs posted on our cubicle or a necklace around our neck that says, "I'm a Christian," but we ought to have some signs that we're connected to the Christ. Signs that manifest in our character. Signs that show up in how we treat and talk to people. When we walk closely with Christ, all the signs that we are His followers will be evident. "Draw nigh to God and he will draw nigh to you" (James 4:8).

FAITH RESPONSE:

DAY 81

"Some trust in chariots, and some in horses: but we will remember the name of the Lord our God."
Psalm 20:7

Whenever I am faced with a difficult situation or a formidable enemy, this psalm registers in my faith file. When I recall to remembrance the strength and power of the Lord our God, I am emboldened with confidence that whatever or whoever I am facing cannot be compared to the power of our God. Our Sovereign is a God of peace and also a God of war; a God who builds and a God who destroys and defends. The very name of our God is enough to cause our enemies to shake. Psalm 62 declares, "God hath spoken once; twice have I heard this: that power belongeth unto God." So, whom shall I fear and of whom shall I be afraid? (Psalm 27)

FAITH RESPONSE:

_____

_____

_____

_____

_____

_____

DAY 82

"And Jabez called on the God of Israel, saying, Oh that thou wouldest bless me indeed, and enlarge my coast, and that thine hand might be with me, and that thou wouldest keep me from evil, that it may not grieve me! And God granted him that which he requested."
1 Chronicles 4:9

Jabez's prayer illustrates two important things. The first is that it is not the length of your prayer but the strength of your prayer that matters. The second is that it is not the eloquence of your words but the substance and sincerity of one's heart. With this one prayer, Jabez redefines his faith and future. He reminds us that we can rise above any life circumstance and live a blessed life. With one prayer you can leave your past behind and break through to an abundance of blessings. Here's the simplicity of his prayer: BLESS ME. When you are blessed, everything and everyone connected to you is blessed. BLESS ME. Is that your prayer? And the Bible says God answered his prayer.

FAITH RESPONSE:

_____

_____

_____

_____

_____

DAY 83

"And it came to pass, that, as they went, they were cleansed."
Luke 17:14b

With all the healing stories in the Bible, this one is unusual. As Jesus entered a village, He was met by ten lepers who were begging for mercy. The compassionate Christ answers their collective prayer and they were given instructions to go show themselves to the priests in the temple. According to the law of Moses, the priests would determine whether they had been healed of leprosy. The ten immediately demonstrate their faith by following Jesus' instruction even though they left His presence with the disease still evident. Their healing did not manifest until they were on their way to the temple. Healing is a process and faith says all is done before seeing any results. Be encouraged. God is working while you are walking.

FAITH RESPONSE:

_____

_____

_____

_____

_____

_____

DAY 84

"Let us not be weary in well doing: for in due season we shall reap if we faint not."
Galatians 6:9

This is Paul's motivational speech to the church at Galatia. He senses this congregation is feeling overwhelmed with the responsibilities of the Christian life and is on the borderline of burnout. Been there, done that! As in the early church, there is still so much work to be done and we rightly conclude we cannot possibly do it all. There are so many needs to meet, so many phone calls to make, so many visitations, so much to burden our finances. All of us, at one time or another, has been on the verge of exhaustion. Perhaps we need to take a step back and assess whether or not we are over-committed and adjust to a schedule that is more reasonable and conducive to maintaining balance in our life. When we do not make this important assessment, we run the risk of a complete depletion of energy and strength. I'm holding out until my due season arrives.

FAITH RESPONSE:

_____
_____
_____
_____
_____

DAY 85

"Fret not thyself because of evildoers, neither be thou envious against the workers of iniquity. For they shall soon be cut down ... Trust in the Lord and do good."
Psalm 37:1-2a; 3

The Hebrew hymn writer gives us the prescription for worry and anxiety. Trust in the Lord and do good and let God handle everything else. When someone does something wrong to us our first instinct is for some "get back." David instructs us not to be concerned with malice-driven people who operate with wicked intent. They feel they need to "cut you down to size" or maybe even they have been self-appointed to "put you in your proper place." The sum total is they are envious of the favor of God that is on your life. Rest in your favor, relax in God's provision, and let God deal with your enemies. The Lord says, "their day is coming."

FAITH RESPONSE:
_____
_____
_____
_____
_____
_____

DAY 86

"... if any would not work, neither should he eat."
2 Thessalonians 3:10b

The caring, maternal nature of a woman is to feed and supply every need, but sometimes we are "woman" to a fault. We overprotect and overcompensate. The wisdom to the church at Thessalonica is wrapped within the matrix of my grandmother's provincial saying: "every tub has to sit on its own bottom." At some point, we have to care enough about ourselves to realize we cannot do it all. We must embrace the notion of everyone carrying their part of the load. The writer is not speaking of people who are physically unable to work or individuals unable to find employment. The problem is with strong bodied individuals who want to live on the graciousness of other people. Today, I watched my sixteen-year-old report for her first day at work. I cried at the realization she will soon be fully independent. Through my tears I smiled, having taught and modeled a principle of work that will last her a lifetime. She will always have something to eat.

FAITH RESPONSE:
_____
_____
_____
_____
_____

DAY 87

"For we know in part..."
1 Corinthians 13:9

I gave my daughter a directive the other day and she responded with the question "Why?" It was a reasonable question given the circumstances. I did not have time for a long explanation, and I responded, "Just do it, and I'll explain later." When it comes to understanding life's experiences and circumstances, sometimes God will explain things to us, and then there are times when God says, "I'll explain later." Romans 8:28 reminds us that God will clear things up later but, be assured God's intent for us is to work all things together for our good. We will always be limited in our understanding of God's activity in our life, but don't be discouraged or fall into despair because you don't have the answer you think you need. Paul reminds us we have limitations. We can only know in part, but God knows the whole story. Tell God exactly what you need and remind yourself GOD KNOWS ALL THINGS AND GOD IS WORKING ON MY BEHALF!

FAITH RESPONSE:

_____

_____

_____

_____

DAY 88

"And Jesus increased in wisdom and stature, and in favor with God and man."
Luke 2:52

This text allows us to get a full panoramic view of the developmental stages of the Christ child and how He connects to the world. Jesus grew in four fundamental areas: intellectually, physically, socially, and spiritually. He was well-adjusted and balanced. Perhaps the lesson for us is that we are also to be balanced; not one-sided, but strong in body, mind, social relationships, and in faithfulness to God.

FAITH RESPONSE:

DAY 89

"And all these blessings shall come on thee, and overtake thee, if thou shalt harken unto the voice of the Lord thy God."
Deuteronomy 28:2; 3-13

The blessings of God are about to overtake you. I can only imagine what it must be like to be assaulted by blessings. That is exactly what the barrage of blessings will look like: an assault. God says these blessings will chase you down. You will be blessed in the city and blessed in the field. The fruit of your body and the fruit of the ground will be blessed. Everything you touch will be blessed. Everywhere you go will be blessed. And then God crowns these magnificent blessings with this: "And the Lord shall make thee the head, and not the tail . . ." Who would not serve a God who can command the blessings of life on you?

FAITH RESPONSE:

_____
_____
_____
_____
_____
_____
_____

DAY 90

"And let them gather . . . in the good years that come, and lay up corn under the hand of Pharaoh."
Genesis 41:35-36

Joseph gives this sound economic advice to Pharaoh that would be helpful for each of us to embrace. It was an economic/financial plan that saved Egypt from the approaching famine. I am teaching my daughter sound financial principles I had to learn and live by. I call them the four S's: share some, save some, spend some, and stretch some.

1) *Share some* is the tithe we set aside for the blessing of the House of God and for our blessing.
2) *Save some* is the tithe we put away in a savings account. It is a disciplined, systematic approach to paying yourself.
3) *Spend some* is a portion of your income for your personal enjoyment because we ought to be good to ourselves.
4) *Stretch some* is how we pay our debts and get out of debt. Stretch yourself by doing without a few things you would like and paying off ALL outstanding debts. "And Pharaoh said of Joseph . . . you are wise" (Genesis 41:39).

FAITH RESPONSE:
_____
_____
_____
_____

ABOUT THE AUTHOR

THE REVEREND DR. KIM Y. NEAL is a native of Brooklyn, New York where she received her formative academic preparation. Her faith journey began with an early acknowledgement of her calling to preach and she has served in a full range of congregational leadership as a senior pastor, executive pastor, associate pastor, and associate minister in her 35 years of servant leadership. Her calling and commitment to preaching the Gospel of Jesus Christ has fueled her gifts as a national evangelist, author and activist, worship leader and worshipper.

Rev. Kim's multi-disciplined education has provided a broad theological landscape for impactful and insightful interpretation of Scripture. Reverend Kim is a subscriber of being a lifetime learner and describes her education as the anchor in the turbulent waters of contemporary culture and contextual ethics. She is a graduate of City College of the City University of the City of New York. She is also a graduate of the dual degree program at Union Theological Seminary in conjunction with Columbia University School of Social Work. Her continuing education led her to American Academy McAllister Institute, also in New York City, where she graduated with a degree in Mortuary Science.

Reverend Kim considers her highest achievement to be the parent of a teenage daughter, Stephanie Nicole. They currently live in Newark, DE. Her life leading Scripture is "what doth the Lord require of thee, but to do justly, and to love mercy, and to walk humbly with thy God?" - Micah 6:8.

www.ingramcontent.com/pod-product-compliance
Lightning Source LLC
Chambersburg PA
CBHW050602300426
44112CB00013B/2034